1 MONTH OF
FREE
READING

at

www.ForgottenBooks.com

By purchasing this book you are eligible for one month membership to ForgottenBooks.com, giving you unlimited access to our entire collection of over 1,000,000 titles via our web site and mobile apps.

To claim your free month visit:

www.forgottenbooks.com/free817240

ISBN 978-0-483-95222-5
PIBN 10817240

THE WORD OF LIFE THE LAW OF MISSIONS.

A

SERMON,

BEFORE THE

AMERICAN BOARD OF COMMISSIONERS FOR FOREIGN MISSIONS,

AT THEIR

MEETING IN BUFFALO, N. Y.

BY

JOSEPH P. THOMPSON, D. D.

PASTOR OF THE BROADWAY TABERNACLE CHURCH, NEW YORK.

BOSTON:
MISSIONARY HOUSE, 33 PEMBERTON SQUARE.
1 8 6 7.

A

SERMON,

BEFORE THE

AMERICAN BOARD OF COMMISSIONERS FOR FOREIGN MISSIONS,

AT THEIR

MEETING IN BUFFALO, N. Y.

BY
JOSEPH P. THOMPSON, D. D.
PASTOR OF THE BROADWAY TABERNACLE CHURCH, NEW YORK.

———————

BOSTON:
MISSIONARY HOUSE, 33 PEMBERTON SQUARE.
1867.

AMERICAN BOARD OF COMMISSIONERS FOR FOREIGN MISSIONS.

BUFFALO, N. Y., OCTOBER, 1867.

Resolved, That the thanks of the Board be presented to the Rev. Dr. THOMPSON, for his Sermon preached on Tuesday evening, and that he be requested to furnish a copy for publication.

Attest,

JOHN O. MEANS, *Rec. Secretary.*

SERMON.

JOHN i. 4.

IN HIM WAS LIFE; AND THE LIFE WAS THE LIGHT OF MEN.

THESE words express the fundamental law of Christian Missions — that the true enlightenment of mankind proceeds from the Life that is in Christ. Our Lord's command to evangelize the nations in his name was but a preceptive form of that Philosophy of Missions which was embodied in his incarnation, and which is at once the constant argument for the missionary work and its deepest inspiration. For whatever the passing type of methods or results in the work of Missions — which vary with epochs of the Church and phases of society — the spiritual condition of mankind that necessitated the incarnation of the divine Word is an unvarying fact of our common humanity, and can be reached only through the life-power that Christ brought into the world.

The coming in of light presupposes a state of darkness; and the darkness in which the light from heaven first appeared was not the accident of one people or age, but a state common alike to the Scythian barbarian, the Greek who had Plato and Aristotle, and the Jew who had Moses and the prophets; a darkness not measured by ignorance alone, but casting its shadow, and even intensifying its gloom, by the side of philosophy, art, culture, and of religion itself —

thus "plucking darkness from the very light;" — a blindness of the heart through its alienation from the life of God. And therefore there was needed not merely the light that comes by shining, *i. e.*, manifestation, discovery, enlightenment, which might come through the progress of science; — but the light that is evolved by Life, *i. e.*, renovation, which can come only from above.

Now, the peculiarity of the light indicated by John, the light of the incarnate Word, was an emanation of Life; "In Him was Life; and the Life was the Light of men." This original philosophy of Missions is the fundamental law on which the work proceeds, and by which our faith and zeal in it must be sustained. The deeper our look into that Philosophy, the firmer our hold upon that Law, the more absolute will be our conviction of duty in the work, the more unwavering our confidence in its results.

Christ who centres in himself Life, Light, and Love, when he allied himself with our Humanity, brought into its sphere a personal power the highest in measure and kind, and of the widest and farthest reach: — for his entering into human flesh was the advent of *Life* and *Light*, the two terms which represent the sum of all power, of all capacity and all blessedness in the universe. He brought to us all that God is, in order that we might become all that man can be.

The text sets forth the personality of the Word as the life-power, and his incarnation as the introduction of that power into the world of mankind for all its generations. The eternal self-subsistence of the Word was the essential prelude to his incarnation, as the incarnation is for us the rendering of his eternal life and love into forms which the human mind can appreciate. "In the beginning was the Word, and the Word was with God, and the Word was God; the same was in the beginning with God."[1] But this conception of the Absolute so far transcends our thought that the evangelist at once descends to the plane of finite, created existence, and links this to the Word as his personal work. "All things were made by Him; and without Him was not anything made that was made:"[2] — the whole universe of matter, life, and mind was conceived in his thought and produced by his act. But we can no more grasp the universe in its totality than existence as an absolute entity; if we attempt to fathom either by our philosophy,

> "The intellect engulphs itself so far,
> That after it the memory cannot go;"[3]

and therefore the Gospel brings the sublime conception with which it opens, still closer to the capacity of our thought. This eternal Word, this absolute and self-sufficient God, this Creator of all things, links himself to this world and to our humanity as the special sphere of his personal manifestation. That we might rise to him, he first came down to us. "The Word was made flesh, and dwelt among us;"[4] he "in whom was life" came into the world to be "the light of men."

These simple words enunciate in the spiritual life that principle of "the correlation of forces" which science has lately suggested as the ultimate law of physical phenomena. As heat will produce motion and motion will generate heat; and again motion in the friction of certain substances will generate electricity, and electricity can be applied to produce mechanical motion, so all forces, it is held, are con-

[1] John i. 1.   [2] John i. 3.   [3] Dante, *Paradiso, Canto* i. 8.   [4] John i. 14.

vertible into each other, and instead of many independent forces, there is one all-pervading *energy*, capable of various transformations in its modes, but indestructible in its nature; in other words, in the operations of nature, nothing is wasted or lost, and nothing wears out; but the energy that seems to be expended in one form, reappears in another.[1] Now this very doctrine of the correlation or the mutual transforming of forces, whose sublime simplicity and almost spiritual insight of the universe place it, even as an hypothesis, among the grandest conceptions of the human mind, was announced eighteen centuries ago as a fundamental principle in the kingdom of spiritual life as constituted by Christ.

On the one hand, Jesus proclaimed himself the "light of the world;" and added, "he that followeth me shall not walk in darkness, but shall have the light of life."[2] Through all the realms of organic nature light is the nourisher of life, "indispensable to a healthy development and a persistent vitality."[3] The chemistry of the sun transmutes inorganic matter into the substances of vegetable growth, distills the fertilizing showers, vitalizes the myriad tribes of insects, evokes the songs of birds, developes in man the red-blood-cells which give body to his muscle, marrow to his bones, and thought to his brain, colors the infant's cheek with the glow of healthy organization, cheers the sick man with healing mercy; in short, the continuance of the physical creation, like its beginning, depends upon the word, "Let there be Light." And here the analogy of the spiritual world at once suggests itself—that Christ in bringing to

---

[1] *The Correlation and Conservation of Forces*, by Professors Grove, Mayer, Faraday and others.

[2] John viii. 12.

[3] *Light; Its Influence on Life and Health*, by Forbes Winslow, M. D., p. 4. See also *Heat as a Mode of Motion*, by Professor Tyndall.

the soul light upon whatever concerns its existence, state, recovery, destiny, as the offspring of God fallen, redeemed, immortal, brings to it a quickening power, the light of *life*.

But on the other hand, the converse is also true, though somewhat less obvious; for Christ was Life as well as Light; and as the light he gave was life to the soul, so the life he imparts is the light of men; and his capacity of giving the kind of light that man's darkness required, and that which distinguishes his light from all other, proceeded from the fact that "in Him was life." Thus did the Gospel anticipate by eighteen centuries the doctrine that science only surmises as a theory, assigning it the place of a fundamental law in the kingdom of Christ. There all forces are correlative, and interchange their functions; Light leads to Life, and Life produces Light, and both emerge in Love. And the Gospel goes back of this subtlest hypothesis of science, — the universal energy, — where science cannot follow, and unveils the one infinite and ineffable PERSON, who is Himself both Life and Light, and the source of all life and light to our souls. There is nothing in the universe so great but Christ is greater. There is nothing so glorious but Christ is more glorious still. And there is no mystery of life, activity, or growth affecting our souls, which is not either revealed in Him, or hidden in Him, who is "the image of the invisible God," who is "before all things," and by whom all forces, principles, beings, laws, visible and invisible, thrones, dominions, principalities, powers, consist or stand together.[1]

The text serves as the nexus of the life of the eternal Word and the life of the historic Christ: it marks the transition from the profound abstractions

[1] Colossians i. 15-18.

of the Prolegomena to the simple narrative of the Gospel — and binds the two together, through the mystic unity of the God-Man. Between the metaphysical formula, "In the beginning was the Word," and the historical formula, "There was a man sent from God, whose name was John," are given the fact of the incarnation, and the necessary reason for it. To men in darkness the eternal Life appeared as the Light "which lighteth every man that cometh into the world;" and John "was sent to bear witness of *that* Light, that all men through him might believe;"[1] and thus the very mystery of the divine life was linked to our personal human life. He who was Life in himself brought Light to man through his life-presence and power. We shall the better comprehend the Incarnation as the philosophy of missions and their fundamental law, if we study the two aspects in which Christ is here presented, Life and Light, first separately, and then in relation to each other.

I. CHRIST WAS LIFE IN HIMSELF, AND THE SELF-SUBSISTING SOURCE OF LIFE TO THE UNIVERSE.

When 1800 years ago a babe was born in Bethlehem of a chaste but lowly virgin, and for want of room in the inn was cradled in a crib of the stable, that tiny and dependent life hid within itself — as yet undeveloped even to Mary's hopeful faith — a life from above, the "power of an endless life." He who entered the world by that lowly portal might have come in a full and perfect manhood, descending from the golden gates swung open, and with a legion of attending angels. But Life and Light come not with observation, and in that very meek and quiet advent lay "the hiding of his power." That "Holy Thing" which was born of Mary was the "Son of God,"[2] "the Word of Life made flesh." Hence in represent-

[1] John i. 7, 8.   [2] Luke i. 35.

ing the birth of Cnrist, all great painters agree in making that new-born life the central light, the radiating glory of the picture. Yet only Raphael, and he but once in a hundred and twenty distinct pictures of the Virgin and child, has succeeded in throwing into the child's eyes the unfathomable pathos of a life, that from some mysterious deep within, looks forth with prophetic yearnings that embrace the whole world, and then dissolve in the eternity beyond;[1]— in him was Life.

(1.) The text affirms of the Word that He has life in himself *independently*. It is not enough that we conceive of him as endowed with life, or as possessing the property of life even from eternity; he *is* the essential Life, underived and absolute. Such a life does not come within any category of human consciousness or observation, but stands apart and alone as the highest conception of being. All life of which we have knowledge is derived and dependent; it springs from some antecedent and exists under certain conditions. Every plant and animal has a beginning, and that beginning proceeds from causes outside of the thing itself, and that were in action before it began to be. Moreover, when life has been produced in a vegetable or animal form, certain laws and conditions must be fulfilled in order to sustain it, and where these fail, the life ceases.

Yet even in this derived and dependent form life is a profound mystery. No scrutiny of science has yet pierced its veil to detect the essential thing called life, apart from the forces and conditions that develop its activity. When life forsakes the body, we cannot see it, touch it, weigh it, photograph its image. "A dead bird weighs as much as a living one. Nothing which our scales can measure is lost when the vital

[1] The Sistine Madonna.

force is gone. It is the Great Imponderable."[1] Nor can all the incantations of our science bid life back again. Having the very same proportions of gelatine, albumen, fat, starch, salt, bone-earth, that enter into the constitution of the human body, we cannot so combine these ingredients as to make a living man; no Liebig has brought forth that product from his laboratory; — even the exact reproduction of the mother's milk which that great chemist had prepared to supply the life-essence of nature's chemistry, turned to poison in the stomach of the babe; and though science has taught us that the action of heat upon the germ, alike in the vegetable and in the animal kingdom, brings forth vital activity, we cannot account for the organizing force in the germ-cell, nor tell how Heat engenders Life.

If then life which we know to be derived and dependent, which had a beginning and can exist only under certain conditions, if this common fact of life in the whole vegetable and animal kingdom is still to us the same dark insoluble mystery that awed the Egyptian four thousand years ago, how stupendous the thought of a life which had no beginning, and is not conditioned upon any facts or laws known to us in the wide universe. Yet such is the thought the text gives us of Christ: — in Him was Life. Life as a principle and a power, Life in its essence, was already in Him, and had been from eternity; and though when he entered into the world he assumed an earthly life under the forms and conditions of humanity, yet could he appropriate without reserve that ineffable title by which Jehovah announced to Moses his absolute and essential being — saying "before Abraham was, I AM;"[2] and again, "I am Alpha and Omega, the beginning and the ending;

---

[1] *The Reign of Law,* by the Duke of Argyle, p. 153.   [2] John viii. 58.

which is and which was, and which is to come, the Almighty."[1] All that pertains to the idea of Life, all that enters into our most refined and most sublime conceptions of God as the absolute and eternal Life, we must transfer to Him who was at once the Son of Man and the Son of God, in order to realize the meaning of the words, IN HIM WAS LIFE.

(2.) But this life which was in Christ in its original and absolute essence, was also *a creative power.* "All things were made by Him, and without Him was not anything made that was made."[2] By virtue of the life-power inhering in his own essential being, he became the author of life to all things that are. Multitudinous and diversified as are the forms of life, from the burning seraph before the throne of God to the glow-worm in the garden, from the angel swift as light to the tiniest insect that creeps and burrows in the dark, from Gabriel loftiest of the sons of God to the infant in its cradle, — all have their existence from Him in whom was Life. This Biblical idea of creation by one personal life-power far transcends the scientific postulate of an all-developing energy in the physical universe. Heat, more nearly than any other force in nature, approximates a spiritual power; for this subtle invisible force is in constant activity throughout the whole creation, now producing motion, now light, now electricity and magnetism, and convertible into every form of force, so that the physical universe may be regarded as one vast factory or laboratory worked by heat. And this grand generalization enables us to comprehend the simplicity and oneness of force amid the many and vast diversities of form. But it stops short of the origin of force, the source of heat or whatever may be the ultimate

---

[1] Rev. i. 8.   [2] John i. 3.

Energy; whereas John's philosophy gives us the One Life-power.

To follow the beautiful illustration of a scientific writer — though all analogies of the material must fail to represent the spiritual — "A cotton factory in full action contains a vast number of machines, many of them but repetitions of one another, but many, too, presenting the most marked diversities in construction, in operation, and in resultant products; for example, one is supplied with the raw material, which it cleans and dresses; another receives the cotton thus prepared, and cards it so as to lay its fibres in such an arrangement as may admit of its being spun; another series, taking up the product supplied by the carding machine, twists and draws it out into threads of various degrees of fineness; and this thread, carried into a fourth set of machines, is woven into a fabric which may be either plain or variously figured, according to the construction of the loom. In every one of these dissimilar operations the *force* which is immediately concerned in bringing about the results is one and the same; and the variety of its products is dependent solely upon the diversity of the material instruments through which it operates. Yet these arrangements, however skillfully devised, are utterly valueless without the force which brings them into play. All the elaborate mechanism, the triumph of human ingenuity in devising, and of skill in constructing, is as powerless as a corpse without the *vis viva* which alone can animate it. The giant stroke of the steam-engine, or the majestic revolution of the water-wheel gives the required impulse; and the vast apparatus which was the moment previously in a state of death-like inactivity, is aroused to all the energy of its wondrous life — every part of its complex organization taking upon itself its peculiar mode of activity, and evolving its own special product, in virtue of the share it receives of the one general force distributed through the entire aggregate of machinery.

"But if we carry back our investigation a stage further, and inquire into the origin of the force supplied by the steam-engine or the water-wheel, we find the agency in each case is Heat: for it is from the heat applied beneath the boiler of the steam-engine that the liquid contained in it derives all its potency as vapor; and, in like manner, it is the heat of the solar rays which pumps up terrestrial waters in the shape of vapor, and thus supplies to man a perennial source of new power in their descent, by the force of gravity, to the level from which they have been raised."[1]

Thus are we led away from the visible mechanism of the factory, from the noisy animation of wheels and spindles back to a silent invisible force that produces all this varied and complicated motion, and without which the whole mechanical structure would be idle and in vain.

But the illustration leaves us still upon the plane of physical forces. It lifts us to the sun, but no higher than the visible heaven in which he moves. To rise where John stood in his contemplation of the divine Word, we must stand with the angel in the sun,[2] we must conceive of a Being who both produced the forms and supplied the forces; who gave to all matter its existence and its modes, who gave to all creatures their life, and who is the first causator and the constant source of all the forces and agencies that sustain nature and produce life; "not circumscribed and all things circumscribing." This personal Christ it was by whom all things were made, without whom was not anything made that was made — for in Him was Life.

[1] Dr. William B. Carpenter.   [2] Rev. xix. i. 7.

(3.) But the analogy of science helps us to a yet higher application of this life-power — *its luminous activity in the sphere of human thought and volition.*

In the great electro-light built for the Northern light-house of the British Government, there is a permanent magnetic power of only sixty pounds in six small stationary magnets; a tiny steam engine that consumes but eighteen ounces of coal per hour, drives an armature in face of these magnets with a velocity of fifteen hundred revolutions per minute, and by the current of electricity thus excited induces.in an electro-magnet of three tons, a dynamic force of electricity that melts iron wire of one quarter inch diameter, so that it drops like molten lead, and flashes forth a light of three times the power of the sun; — heat passes into motion, motion into magnetic electricity, and this again into light and heat a thousand times intensified. But all these forces lay dormant until intelligence combined them; and so all the divine powers of the soul, and the luminous properties of truth were latent and dormant, till the Life came and kindled them into Light.

The ideas of self-subsistence and of creative power do not exhaust the meaning of these four monosyllables, "In Him was Life." The work of the material creation, in which light was the most efficient agent, was typical of that spiritual creation wherein Christ by his own life-power doth make all things new. It was for the work of this creation that "the Word was made flesh and dwelt among us, full of grace and truth;" and "as many as received Him, to them gave he power to become the sons of God."[1] In Him was life as *the restorative power for the world of mankind,* made dark and dead by sin. The soul that separates itself from God, by that act is dead unto all the

---

[1] John i. 12.

spiritual ends, powers, joys, for which it was created a personal intelligence. It has no activity of thought, will, affection toward the objects for which a being made in God's image should think, live, and act, but powers given for a spiritual and immortal life are wasted in the service of sense, upon objects of earth and time. And thus the whole race of man was dead in trespasses and sins; "having the understanding darkened, being alienated from the life of God through the ignorance that is in them, because of the blindness of their heart."[1]

This condition, though utterly abnormal in the contemplation of a sound philosophy of mind, was the universal and invariable fact of human experience, a fact of uniform sequence, and therefore *a law of history*—not in the sense in which Positivists apply the term law to the phenomena of society, as a uniformity "with which no volitions either natural or supernatural interfere"[2]—but what Mr. Stuart Mill himself describes as "simple invariability of sequence, without any mysterious compulsion;"[3] a law in fact resulting from the concurrence of mankind in willfully and therefore guiltily departing from God; — "they are all gone out of the way, they are together become unprofitable; there is none that seeketh after God."[4]

Such being the law of human history, and all the more because the common stream of depravity was made up of the several but confluent rills of personal volition, — its whole set toward the sea of death, — there was no hope of counteraction but through the interference of a "supernatural volition" (I accept the term of the Positivist) — even a volition of divine pity and mercy seeking to save the lost. Into the

---

[1] Ephesians iv. 18. [2] Auguste Comte, *Positive Philosophy.*
[3] Examination of Sir William Hamilton's Philosophy, vol. 2, p. 300.
[4] Romans iii. 12.

world of spiritual darkness and death there must come a Life-Power from above, a Power greater than the soul, and adequate to compass its condition and necessities, a Power knowing how to reach the soul through its own nature, and, in the delicate and sensitive sphere of moral causes, to change the law of action without impairing the acting-power — the personality of the soul itself; a Power to quicken, enlighten, renew, restore, by bringing the soul again into its true and normal relations with God, and by bringing God nigh to the soul, that his presence, his truth, his holiness, his love, might act upon it as realities. Christ embodying the truth, the righteousness and the love of God in a living expression that men could see and feel, and bringing home to their hearts the reconciling grace of God by the sacrifice of himself upon the cross, was this life-power — a Power which, having in the Atonement gained a leverage against the law of sin and death, can move the world; and which moving ever from that fulcrum, carries on through the ages the work of restoration, till reversing the old law of history it shall make all things new.

This personal transforming power of Christ within the sphere of Humanity, is no less a wonder of Redemption, whose out-come it is, than is his official or priestly work of atonement for sin; "for if, when we were enemies, we were reconciled to God by the death of his Son, much more being reconciled, we shall be saved by his *life*." [1] The Incarnation brought that life into contact with our sin-bound, sin-deadened world as an abiding power; for though the personal life of Christ is now simply a matter of record in the Gospel, its spirit has entered into history through the Church, as the most positive, permanent, purifying

[1] Romans v. 10.

and progressive power in modern civilization, and its light remains to "lighten every man that cometh into the world." "The law was given by Moses," and the law worked only death; but "grace and truth came by Jesus Christ,"[1] "the law of the spirit of life,"[2] for "in Him was life."

II. But the text recalls us to THE ILLUMINATING POWER OF THE LIFE THAT WAS IN CHRIST. A light he was obviously in the external relations of teacher and guide, giving certainty to knowledge in respect to spiritual things, and opening paths untrodden by reason in its endeavors after truth. But the meaning of John lies deeper. The incarnate Word was "*the* Light of men," "the true Light," the light adapted to man's condition of darkness and sin; the light which only could dispel a darkness caused by sin. And such a Light he was by virtue of the Life that was in him; for whereas his shining was unto life, the Light of Life, so by the principle of correlation, the Life was the Light of men.

The philosophical relation of Life to Light leads us back to the source of all things. It is the nature of Life to manifest itself; and since "whatsoever doth make manifest is light," the power or quality of making manifest is the very essence of light. Thus a fire-fly makes itself visible in the dark by the light which it emits through the action of its own vital powers; and a visibility caused by the object seen is manifestation or light in its highest form. God is Life; and this absolute Life was first in the order of thought; but the manifestation of this Life through creation and to intelligent creatures was Light — the Life passing into Light by its tendency to make itself manifest. In the spiritual world Christ as Life becomes the Light of men by making Himself mani-

---

[1] John i. 17.   [2] Romans viii. 2.

3

fest to the soul, and by leading the soul to the manifestation of its true life in Him.

(1) As the absolute and eternal Life, and the giver of life to all creatures, *Christ holds clearly in his view the whole universe of thought and of fact,* and therefore can light this up as the sun lights up the material worlds. He knows all things, since all things were made by him; he knows where lie truth and right, and where error and wrong; he knows what is in man, and as the Son of God, he knows what is in God. "No man hath seen God at any time; the only begotten Son, which is in the bosom of the Father, he hath declared him."[1] As the absolute Life, he was the infallible revealer of God, and of the realities of that spiritual and eternal world from which he came into the world of sense and time. He, "the blessed and only Potentate, the King of kings, and Lord of lords, who only hath immortality, dwelling in the light which no man can approach unto,"[2] brought "life and immortality to light" by his appearing.

What light shone upon the nature of God, when the Word, veiled in human flesh, proclaimed "God is a spirit, and they that worship Him must worship Him in spirit and in truth."[3] What light shone upon the character of God, when this Holy and Just One, who went about doing good, declared "he that hath seen me hath seen the Father."[4] What light shone upon the power of God, when "as the Father raiseth up the dead and quickeneth them,"[5] even so the Son raised Lazarus by his word. What light shone upon the grace of God, when his only-begotten Son, himself dying for the sins of men, offered eternal life to all who would believe in his name. And oh, what light shone upon the future of man — where Socrates had dimly hoped, and after four hundred years Cicero

[1] John i. 18. [2] 1 Tim. vi. 15, 16. [3] John iv. 24. [4] John xiv. 9. [5] John v. 21.

had doubted still — when the Son of Man, crucified and buried, rose in the power of an endless life and ascended to heaven, saying "I go to prepare a place for you;" and again, "every one which seeth the Son, and believeth on him, hath everlasting life; and I will raise him up at the last day."[1] In all the momentous facts concerning man as a spiritual being, Christ was the Light of men, because in Him was Life.

(2) And this Life is the light of men, because *by quickening its perception of spiritual things, and the activity of its moral powers, Christ brings the Soul to discern and receive the truth.* 'Tis no use, the sun shining upon a dead man. He lies there stark, cold, blind, insensible to light or heat. And one dead in sin would see no light of truth, though the heavens were written all over with the name of God.

"The light of the body is the eye," but it must be a sound, living eye; for, as Coleridge says, "detach the eye from the body; behold it, handle it, with its various accompaniments or constituent parts, of tendon, ligament, membrane, blood-vessel, gland, humors; its nerves of sense, of sensation, and of motion. Is this cold jelly the light of the body? Is this what you mean when you describe the eye as the telescope and the mirror of the soul, the seat and agent of an almost magical power?"[2] No; the eye must be a living organ, or there is no light, though all creation were ablaze. A purely intellectual revelation disclosing God as an object of philosophic thought, could not have sufficed to enlighten the world. Its light would have gone out in the surrounding darkness; or at best, it would have been like moonlight upon a world wrapped in snow, making the cold seem colder still, and the firmament to crackle with icy spar. There must be life to make the light perceptible or pleasur-

---

[1] John vi. 40, and xiv. 2.   [2] *Aids to Reflection*, Conclusion.

able; and therefore, the soul must be quickened in its moral feelings before it will take the full meaning and enjoy the full benefit of the truth that Christ reveals. The elementary truths of "repentance for sin" and "faith toward God," must first strike the heart, and by quickening the moral nature prepare the way for the higher truths; and thus by awakening conscience, arousing sensibility, and moving the heart with love, Christ lets in upon the soul the full light of his glory. This correlation of life and light explains that otherwise anomalous saying of Paul, "Awake thou that sleepest and arise from the *dead*, and Christ shall give thee *light*." The analogy of thought would seem to require "life," a higher life to be imparted by Christ, as the crown of the sentence; but his life-power leads to light, and only the soul awakened by his spirit to receptivity can enter into that light which shall be its life forevermore. We see because we live, and seeing live alway. "In Him was Life and the Life was the Light of men."

The doctrine of the text finds already strong confirmation in history, and is yet to have its full verification in the renovation of the world through the Gospel.

I. *The incarnation of Christ marks the epoch of a new civilization, through the enlightenment of mankind for a true and perfectible life.* It is just now the cue of a sect of materialists — for there are sects in science as in religion, and dogmatism, speculation, heresy as well — to run back the origin of man to a dateless antiquity, and a condition of degradation close upon the brute, and then to derive from his history a natural law of development that would exclude the idea of intervention through a divine revelation. The alleged data upon which this hypothesis is based are as yet too few and indeterminate to warrant a scientific statement concerning the *origines* of human history; but whatever may be the final result in respect to chronology and the condition of the race in prehistoric times, nothing can change the historical fact, that the Christian era marks the creation of a new world in ideas and in morals, in intellectual and in social life.

I freely concede — and as a believer in the Christian Revelation, most gladly accept — all that Humanity had attained before that epoch ; — the material grandeur of the old civilization in Egypt and Assyria, the graceful and splendid culture of the later civilization in Greece and Rome; its potency in Art, in Literature, and in Philosophy, holding the thought of all after ages in its spell. Yet the fact remains that the civilized world has not simply outgrown but has *discarded* its type of human society. That old civilization is traced by the scholar in fragments and remains; it is parcelled out among the British Museum, the Louvre, the Vatican, the museums of Berlin, Florence, Leyden, Naples, Petersburg, Turin, Vienna, and lesser collections of antiquities in palaces and academies of the old world, and in college-halls of the new; its influence survives in Language and Letters, in the Platonic and Aristotelian methods that forever divide the empire of Metaphysics, in forms of Beauty and canons of Taste, and in Customs and Laws that linger beyond the memory of their origin; but nowhere does it exist as a concrete and palpable power. The old world died of moral inanition. One may read the verdict in the Annals of Tacitus, the Epistles of Seneca, the Satires of Juvenal, and on the uncovered walls of Pompeii. The old civilization failed of two essential conditions; — the improvement of the masses, and the enthronement of virtue by the sanctions of law and of public sentiment.

But Christianity, limited and imperfect as has been its application hitherto, marks the rise of Humanity itself, through the recognition of the individual man as the subject of personal rights and of commensurate responsibilities; through the enfranchisement of woman as the subject of prerogative and honor — above the competition of majorities for labor and rights — to be cherished and defended by a sacred chivalry, in the higher sphere of the esthetic sentiments;[1] through the conservation of the family as the sanctuary of love and purity, and the true unit of society and the state; through the exaltation of the public good as the end of government; through the ennobling of the soul as redeemed and immortal, and the commending of the poor as children of the all-loving Father, before whom all are brethren. From such ideas and their spirit leavening communities, have sprung the great universities of learning, the purest schools of art, the most just and liberal governments, the most wise and equal laws, institutions of charity and reform, of industrial order and progress; — in a word, all that pertains to the improvement of mankind as a whole in knowledge, virtue, happiness, which is the highest type of civilization, is a growth of the Christian era, and flourishes best where Christianity is most free and pure and strong.

The Jew dated events from the creation — "the year of the world;" the Roman from the founding of the city; but the city as he made it is gone, and the world itself now dates from Christ, the true unit or norm of Humanity, about whom crystallize all the elements of a worthy history — whose subject is Mankind, and whose law the Moral Order of Society. By his coming there entered into the world not only new light but a new power. For since the light from him

---

[1] Eph. v. 25. 1 Peter iii. 7.

sprang of the life that was in him, his incarnation was a two-fold birth; of the divine into the human, of the human unto the divine; the birth of a new world out of darkness through the Life that was the Light of men.

II. *The Church of Christ is the organic medium of his light, and in the measure in which it shares his life, becomes the light of the world.* The light of the Saviour's life and teaching that is spread over the pages of the New Testament becomes concentrated in the Church — the Communion of saints — making that luminous as the body of Christ, whose holy and blessed one-ness in Him and the Father is the abiding witness for the divine mission and work of the Lord Jesus. Other associations may be organized for the purpose of spreading light upon special topics, — like the Smithsonian Institution "for the diffusion of knowledge among mankind," — or for exerting influence in a given direction, as societies for specific reforms. But the Church of Christ is organically a luminous body; a city set on a hill, which cannot be hid. It shines because it exists; but it exists, and therefore shines, only when its " life is hid with Christ in God."

To the disciples whom he would leave behind him to represent his life and doctrine among men, Jesus said, " Ye are the light of the world." And this was said of a little company of obscure men — fishermen, small farmers, here and there a publican, a few women in humble life, the poor of a subjugated and despised race, not a priest, a scholar, or a ruler among them — for as yet there was not in their whole circle so much of human learning as the Apostle Paul afterwards brought to the illustration of the Christian faith, and though Nicodemus and Joseph of Arimathea had been secretly drawn to Jesus, they had not avowed

Him as the Messiah; — of such unlettered, untitled, uninfluential men, with absolutely no position and no prospect in the world, was it said, they were not simply a light to their sect, their times, their country, but *the* light of the world. And how marvellously has this declaration been fulfilled in five of that little band, Matthew, Mark, John, Peter, and James, who have given to the world more of the light of truth and holiness than all the wisdom of the ancients had been able to produce. And wherever now the light of knowledge, truth, virtue shines brightest and purest, there the Gospels and Epistles of those primitive disciples are the fountain and the glory of that light. So penetrated were they with the life of Christ that by reproducing Him, — the Incarnate Word, the atoning Saviour, the risen Lord, — they have become the transparencies through which his image shines; and whatever the form of outward representation, we see in all the living Christ. Not the veil of St. Veronica which in wiping the brow of Jesus on his way to Calvary, caught his sacred features, not the cloth which our Lord sent to the king of Edessa with his own perfect portrait, and which by its miraculous light photographed itself upon the very walls of cities, not any ideal of Christ that legend has invented or art produced, could so represent the Son of Man as do the evangelists, who do not once describe, nor so much as hint at his human features. It was the life of Jesus infused into their souls that caused them to glow with the light of his countenance; "for the life was manifested," saith John, "and we have seen it, and bear witness, and show unto you that eternal life, which was with the Father, and was manifested unto us."[1]

And every soul that receives Christ as its life becomes transparent with his image, and according to

[1] 1 John i. 2.

its sphere an enlightener of mankind: and so the Church — not as represented by organization, sacraments, forms, structures, officers, rituals, councils, creeds, though these all have their intermediate functions — but the Church as constituted of living disciples, true to their faith, true to their Lord, true to their stewardship of the manifold grace of God, true to their commission to evangelize the nations, the Church of renewed, praying, living souls is the light of the world — the light as they receive and manifest the life; for the Scriptures, again affirming the sublime spiritual law of correlation, declare that these "shine as lights in the world, holding forth the word of life."[1]

III. *The Christianizing of the world, which is the necessary means to the perfection of human society, must be accomplished by carrying the life of Christ to the souls of individual men, through the Gospel of his grace, undiluted, unperverted and unpatronized!* It is pretty much conceded that the Christian religion in some form is to become the prevailing faith of mankind, and that the type of civilization known as Christian is destined to overspread the world. Even those speculative Progressionists who regard Christianity as but a normal type of belief, which was developed in its turn and has now served its time, will patronize this antiquated and expiring system as the best hitherto produced, and while according it a decent sepulture, will condescend to borrow from it certain germs of thought for the development of their more sublimated theism and more spiritualized ethics; while in their theory of human perfectibility, they cannot advance beyond the Gospel ideal of holiness and the Gospel rule of love.

One of the most pure and earnest advocates of that

---

[1] Phil. ii. 15.

school which rejects the historical revelation of Christianity as a "Book-religion," and seeks to found the Faith of the Future as a "religion of the Absolute," upon the "revelation of consciousness,"[1] naively presents self-consecration, in love to God and man, as the highest development of religion in the soul, makes it "the duty of man to give to the love of God the highest place in his heart," and argues that under this consecration "religion would be the living heart of such a life"—a life dedicated "without reservation forever to be a life in God and for God"—and "the man's whole possessions, time, talents, worldly wealth would be held by him as things whereby he could do God's work in the world." Such a consecration, moreover, we are told, "will teach us to feel that there is no human being below the level of our sympathies," will make us "feel *especially* for all the degraded," and love and serve those who in themselves are most unlovely.

But these truths so forcibly propounded as the latest discoveries of the Absolute Religion and the ultimate truths of consciousness, are only a reflection from that Book-religion which has governed the Church of Christ for 1800 years; nor would any human consciousness ever have developed them into a law of life but through the life-power that is in the Book. For there we find these self-same truths, not simply written in sentences, but incarnated as a human personality in Him whose life is the light of men. And so the highest outcome of philosophic Theism brings us back to Christianity as the hope of the world. There is a something in this Christ too lofty and commanding to admit of being patronized by the expounders of "the Absolute"—a "consciousness of humanity" more

---

[1] See *Religious Duty*, and *Broken Lights*, by Miss Frances Power Cobbe.

profound, an intuition of divinity more absolute than theirs.

The question of the regeneration of society is therefore practically the question, 'What type of Christianity shall be impressed upon unevangelized nations, or in what form shall Christianity be applied to the restoration of the world?' The Bishop of Natal answers 'only a *rationalized* Christianity will suit an intelligent and inquisitive Zulu, versed in the arithmetic of Jacob's sons and the mensuration of the ark.' 'No,' retorts the Lord Bishop of Honolulu, 'not a rationalistic but a *ritualistic* Christianity will win the simple children of nature, by making Christian sacraments and worship a refinement upon the sacred rites of their ancestors, and thus appealing to their old religious sentiment, without Puritanic harshness.'

Our answer is, neither Gerizim nor Jerusalem, but Christ; — that Christianity will give the true light which itself comes nearest to the Life; and the true evangelization is not primarily by an external apparatus for illumination, whether literary or ecclesiastical, but the preaching of the Gospel with a view to its direct living, saving power upon the souls of men; and all the machinery of missions, — organization, publication, boards, societies, schools, churches, — must be subservient to this life-knowledge of Christ in the soul, or it becomes an obstruction to the light; for no one can come to the full light of Christianity who has not received a new life of his soul through the quickening, illuminating, renovating life of Christ. For lack of that inward receiving of Christ, the light may shine in darkness and the darkness comprehend it not. If in any land our missions lack success, it is not for lack of organization, or science or ceremony, but solely for lack of the life — and this chiefly the lack of a living prayerful union with Christ in the

Church here, vitalizing the work yonder, and flashing light through wires that never break nor falter, that cross every continent and fathom every sea. More light of science for the African! more light of candles for the Islander! nay, more of that life which has already in one generation created a Christian people of the barbarians of the Pacific, and at the same time, in Turkey, has formed a commonwealth of intelligent, spiritual, practical believers, out of captious and ritualistic orientals.

If we would see the light of Christianity spread in our time, we must lay *our* Christianity nearer to the Life. Appeals to sensibility pall by repetition. Appeals for money have already exhausted the ingenuity and rhetoric of secretaries, agents and pastors. Appeals for men meet no response when there is no moving impulse within the Church. The romance of the missionary enterprise is gone; even its heroism is challenged by adventurous travelers and explorers. Arguments for missions from statistical results, from commercial benefits, from social progress, from motives of philanthropy, while they increase in weight with years, decline in power through familiarity; and even the picture of the vices and miseries of the heathen fails to stir the heart, if too often photographed to the eye. Luxury grows apace; riches increase, and with them desires, tastes, gratifications; while the Mission-Board is regarded as an insurance to be kept up at a fixed rate of premium, an annual assessment for which increase of income is not reckoned! Ah, brethren, would we see the light of the Gospel advancing, we must lift ourselves to the height of the great argument of the text; must feel the power of an endless life; must have within us the life of Christ, yearning with possibilities of good so vast and glorious, that it will not permit us to be satisfied in working, giving, or accomplishing, till He shall be satisfied of the travail of his soul. Our first want is never Learning, nor Wealth, nor Measures, nor Men, but more of that LIFE, which in the work of missions is the law of progress and of power. "In Him was life; and the life was the light of men;" and we are sent to bear witness of *that* Light — and *none other* — "that all men through him might believe."

It is nothing that the Light is come, unless we have the Life. One may shut himself up in a darkened laboratory to analyze a ray of the sun admitted through one little aperture; he may measure its force and velocity, produce the spectrum and ascertain the properties of each color blended in the solar beam; yet should he persistently engage in this process of analyzing light, his own system the while would pine and shrivel for lack of the life-power, the blood-power, of the sun. And one may so deal with Christianity as an intellectual text-book, with its facts and doctrines as matter of critical analysis, with Christ himself as a historical or mythical phenomenon, with the Gospel as a subject for the microscope, as utterly to miss the life-power of Christ warming and enlightening the soul. And this is what Rationalism would accomplish for an inquisitive Zulu: give him a light, without actinism, a Christianity without life.

On the other hand, the very agency appointed for giving light may be made a means of impeding its vitality. The moon which is hung as a mirror to reflect the sun upon our night may swing round so as to hide the sun by day. Should that eclipse be prolonged, the earth would grow chill under its pallor; all warmth and vitality would by and by be gone; vegetable life would grow sickly and decay; the brute creation would go wild with terror, and with melancholy howlings die. It was thus that in the middle ages the Church, constituted to be the light of the world, obtruded its hierarchy and ritual before the Word of life. And a ritualistic Christianity is but the intervention of artificial lights by which the true is cast into the shadow. Like the Athenian worship in the time of Pericles, it is " an attempt to relieve the mind by the daily amusement of its sacrifices." In its culmination at Rome on the 29th of June last, it illumined the interior of St. Peter's with its hundred thousand candles, whose twinkling was made visible by curtaining off the light of the sun from the dome and windows. And this is what Ritualism would accomplish for the sunny islands of the Pacific — curtain off the day that its wax-tapers might be seen!

Ah, man still, as at the first, has need of the light of life, for his darkness is of a character which only Life can penetrate and absorb. Upon the shortest day of the year I stood within the Cathedral of the Assumption at Moscow, the most sacred sanctuary of the Greek Church. In local associations this is even more impressive than St. Peter's, while its dimensions are more easily mastered, and the unity of its effect is neither lost in vastness nor broken by side-chapels that dispute the preeminence of sanctity and riches. Here the Chief Patriarch has his seat. Here all former Patriarchs lie buried. Here is the holy chrism which, reproduced like the oil of the widow of Sarepta, is applied in baptism to every child born within the pale of the Greek Church throughout the Empire. Here every Emperor of Russia for four hundred years has taken the oath and received the sacrament of coronation. Here Byzantine art has decorated the walls, pillars, and ceiling, with the whole history of the Gospel and the Church, in gold and enamel; while imperial magnificence and passionate devotion have lavished upon altars, shrines, and pictures.

> " The wealth of Ormus and of Ind,
> Barbaric pearl and gold."

The service was majestically intoned by a celebrant who looked the very king of priests; and splendid choral responses rolled their deep-voiced bass under the spray of boys' voices, richer than organ or lute. At the close of the Litany, when the golden gates of the *Iconostasis*[1] swung open, and the Holy of Holies appeared glittering with gems and wreathed with incense, the sunlight stole in through the domes, heightening the effect of candles, till all the jewels were ablaze, and the four walls, gilded and painted from floor to roof, were resplendent as an apocalyptic vision; — on the altar-screen the Eternal Father, the Virgin and the Son, with patriarchs, prophets, angels and apostles in gold and brilliants; on the right wall the seven holy Councils; on the left the story of the Virgin's life; on the pillars the canonized martyrs; in front the last judgment, — all history represented as related to Christ; the cathedral one grand and solemn Te Deum, the goodly fellowship of the prophets, the noble army of martyrs, the glorious company of the apostles praising the King of glory, who will come to be our Judge. Of a sudden the sun kindled the halo around the infant Saviour upon the Altar-screen, and for an instant all the light of the Cathedral was beaming from his face. It seemed to say, This brilliancy of color, gold, and jewels is not light; there is no warmth in these walls, no life-power in this ritual; Life only can give light; and "I AM COME THAT YE MIGHT HAVE LIFE."

[1] The *Iconostasis* is a screen covered with sacred pictures, which shuts off the *Bema* or Sanctuary from the congregation.

CPSIA information can be obtained
at www.ICGtesting.com
Printed in the USA
BVHW090721081118
532427BV00011B/623/P